Try Not To Laugh Challenge™ Joke Book

WhipperSnapper Edition

PRIZES!

$50 GIFT CARD

Think YOU can win our JOKE CONTEST?!?!

Try Not to Laugh Challenge is having a CONTEST to see who is the MOST HILARIOUS boy or girl in the USA.

Please have your parents email us your best **original** joke and you could win a $50 gift card to Amazon.

Here are the rules:

1. It must be funny. Please do not give us jokes that aren't funny. We get enough of those from our joke writers

2. It must be original. We have computers and we know how to use them.

3. No help from the parents. Plus, they aren't even that funny anyway!!

Email your best joke to:

 tntlpublishing@gmail.com

Winners will be announced via email.

Try Not to Laugh Challenge Group

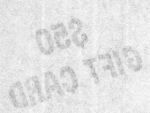

PRIZES!

$50 GIFT CARD

STOP

Please have your parents email us your best "original" joke and you could win a $50 gift card to Amazon.

The Try Not To Laugh ™ Challenge Instructions:

- Face your opponent.

- Take turns reading jokes out loud to each other. HINT: Funny faces & noises are fair game!

- When someone laughs the other person gains a point.

- Person to get to 3 points is named The Try Not to Laugh CHAMPION!

Why was the electron always feeling sad?

Because he was so negative.

What type of underwear is always getting in fights?

Boxers.

Where was the basketball's trial?

The court.

How did the mailman hurt his head?

He ran into a post.

What is a volcano's favorite dessert?

Lava cake!

Knock Knock.
Who's there?
Woodchuck.
Woodchuck who?
I wouldn't chuck anybody. That's rude.

What does Christopher say when he meets a new lady?

"Call me Chris, miss."

How come Clarence the Clam wouldn't share his toys?

Because he was a little shellfish.

Why do Almonds make such bad neighbors?

Because they're nuts!

What did the clock say to
the garbage can?
Stop wasting your time!

What do you call a fishing pole
lost at sea?
A cast-away.

Why can't a chicken pitch in baseball?
Because he bawks!

Why did the plane park in the closet?
It needed a hangar!

What is more daring than a rock?
A boulder.

How did the Detective know Quasimodo
was guilty?
Because he had a hunch!

What's a river's favorite way
to watch TV?
Streaming!

What did the cop say to the blanket?
Cover me!

What did the pirate wish he was instead?
An aye doctor

Why could the car finally relax?
It was re-tired

Why did the basketball player run away from his breakfast?
Because he was on a fast break.

Why did the corn stalk ask the farmer to repeat everything he said?
The corn stalk had only one ear.

What did the seedling call its father?
Poppyseed.

What is the worst type of cup to pour hot tea into?
A buttercup.

Why did the yeast stop telling jokes to the bread?
He couldn't get a rise out of her.

What do people in France like to eat with eggs?

French toast!

Who won the race between a sausage and two eggs?

The eggs. They scrambled to the finish.

What kind of food goes down hills the fastest?

A dinner roll.

How did the monkeys escape the zookeeper after stealing bananas?

They dropped some peels and gave him the slip.

Why did the earthquake rattle the ice cream?

Because he ordered a shake!

What did the Englishman want for breakfast?

Cheerio-s!

Why did the butter keep telling jokes?

He was on a roll

Who is winning the vegetable race?

Last I heard, the tomato was a head of lettuce.

What does a tomato have on his feet?

Toma-toes.

What kind of ring does a man like best?
Onion rings!

Which baseball player can carry
the most water?
The pitcher.

What did the foot say to his mom when
he got in a fight at school?
"But mom, he socked me!"

What do a quarterback and a pilot
have in common?
Touchdowns!

Why couldn't the basketball coach
ever find his wallet?
He always left it all out on the court.

Why did the knight use poison instead of his sword to kill the mythical winged, fire-breathing creature?

He didn't want the fight to drag-on.

Why isn't "Werewolf" spelled with an "H"?

No one wants to scream "Herewolf"!

What does a corn spider spin?

Cobwebs.

What does a cat in pain say?

Me-ow!

What is a tree's favorite drink?

Root beer.

Which animal loves the Pansy flower?

Chimpanzee!

What type of bees do dogs love to catch?

Frisbees.

How do you know when two spiders get married?

They tie the knot.

What do crocodiles cook with?

Crockpots!

What do dust bunnies use to cook their meals?

Dustpans!

What's a pitcher's favorite jewel?
A diamond.

What are the best kinds of mistakes to
make in basketball?
Alley-oops.

What happens when you leave an icicle?
You get a BYEcycle.

What's a dancer's favorite drink?
Tap water.

Why aren't birds allowed
to play basketball?
They commit too many fowls.

Why did the Kit-Kat split in two?
It needed a break.

How does a broken plate laugh?
It cracks up.

"Where I come from, we are all considered the smartest!", said the Orange Juice. "And where would that be?", Asked the Apple Juice. Orange Juice replied, "I'm from Concentrate."

Why did the butter keep telling jokes?
He was on a roll.

Why couldn't Pepper go to lunch with Salt?
He was grounded.

What's a golfer's favorite number?

Foooooooooour!

The tennis racket was concerned that
the tennis ball would never be the same
after surgery. What did the tennis ball
have to say about that? "Don't worry,
I'll bounce back!"

Why did the boy take off his baseball
glove when he went out in the snow?

Because he didn't want to catch a cold.

What did the baseball player do when an
acid-spitting monster was chasing him?

He ran to the base.

The Bearded Lady from the circus went to the pet store to buy a pet. What did she buy?

A bearded dragon.

When the camel asked for sugar with his tea, what did the waitress ask?

"One hump or two?"

Why won't the star basketball player go to haunted houses?

Because he always starts.

Why did the baseball player stop bowling?

He had three strikes

Why did the man get fired from the calendar store?
He took a day off

What award does the dentist of the year get?
A little plaque

What did the fireman do when the policeman made fun of him?
He went to a burn clinic.

Why did the dalmatian suddenly run away?
He realized he had been spotted.

Why did the policeman walk
into the bar?
Because he forgot to duck!

Why doesn't anyone invite the
hog over for dinner?
Because he's such a pig.

Why do lightbulbs get such good grades?
Because they're so bright.

What does a planet say when it wants
to be left alone?
"I need more space."

What did the tree say when he broke
up with his girlfriend?
"I'm going to leaf you."

What did the police officer say to the
snowman who was robbing a bank?
"Freeze!"

Why was the shark given a promotion?
He took a big bite out of his competition.

What is a hand's favorite type of plant?
A palm tree.

Why couldn't the astronaut
ever pay attention?
She was always spacing out.

Why did the 50 cents not want
to be broken up?
They were close quarters

What did the egg do when he saw
his friend fall?
He cracked up

How come the broken pencil couldn't
answer the question?
It drew a blank

What do you call a well-dressed lion?
A dandy-lion

Why was the rest of the furniture
scared of the bookshelf?
It had a few loose screws

What does a cloud wear to dress up
for a party?
A rain bow-tie.

What does everyone say about the
mountain who can play the guitar?
"He's a real rock star."

What did the stick of gum say to the
other before a fight?
"You want a piece of me?"

What did the beach ask the ocean?
"Water you doing today?"

What happens when shoelaces
fall in love?
They tie the knot

Why did the desk keep winning?
It was luck of the drawer

Why didn't the forest get the
desert's joke?
Because it was too dry.

Why didn't the van want to sleep inside?
It was a camper

Why don't steak knives like hanging out
with butter knives?
Because they're so dull.

How do lizards always know
their own weight?
Because they are covered with scales.

What do you call it when two pieces
of fruit stop dating?
A banana split.

What animal is the best at
stopping leaks?
A seal.

When does a clock go to the dentist?
When its tooth-thirty

Why was the cardboard so bad
at poker?
It was a folder

What happened when the foot splashed
in the puddle?
It got the boot

What do you call a broken watch?
A waste of time

What happened when the apples
got married?
They lived apple-y ever after

Why can't you trust a clock with
your secrets?
Because time will tell

Why didn't the chalkboard take a bath?
It was a clean slate

Why was the shoe so nice to everyone?
It had a good sole

Why do teachers always put the skeleton
in the corner?
They are bad to the bone

Why couldn't the band go on a cruise?
You shouldn't rock the boat

What is a writer's favorite place
to sleep?
An alpha-bed

Why did the cloud love the snowflakes?
They're down to Earth

Why was the saxophone working out?
To be as fit as the fiddle

Why is the Hulk growing a garden?
He has a green thumb

Who always gets ripped off from
the store?
The price tag

How did the sun get so many planets?
It gave them a warm welcome

What happens when a sausage has .
a bad dream?
Your wurst nightmare

Why were the sheep waiting at the
end of the alphabet?

To catch some z's

Why did the magician only ask
for a penny?

It was a cheap trick

Why did the conductor put a
trampoline on the train?

So you can jump aboard

Why was everyone impressed when
the fish played the piano?

It was a good tuna

Why couldn't the bird make a decision?
He was always on the fence.

Why can you always trust a mouse?
Cause he ain't no rat!

How do elephants get ready for
a vacation?
They pack their trunk.

What is a golfer's favorite kind of bird?
An eagle.

.

My dog's on vacation.
He's staying at a Collie-Day Inn.

What do you call a frog that lives
alone in a cave?
Hermit the Frog

What kind of flower is a mistake?
Whoops-a-daisy!

What's more fun than a barrel full of
monkeys?
Just about anything. Who wants a barrel
full of monkeys?

Who's the most popular fish
in the ocean?
The Starfish

Why did old MacDonald's son get a
bad grade in spelling?
He thought farm was spelled E-I-E-I-O

What did one sausage say to the other sausage?

Let me be frank.

How come the penguin didn't show up for his date?

He got cold feet.

Why were the cowboys firing their guns in the air?

They were just shooting the breeze.

Why did the kid attach wheels to his mom's fruit bowl?

He was trying to drive her bananas.

What does a ghost call a cut on its finger?

A boo-boo

What is the noisiest kind of cookie?
A ginger snap.

What part of an egg is the cleanest?
The white.

Why did the tortilla chip go to
the pool party?
It wanted to take a dip.

What do you call a cow taking a nap?
Ground beef.

When did the secretive grape
spill everything?
When it went to the press.

What is a fashion designer's favorite
kind of chips?
Ruffles.

Why can't icebergs tell jokes?
They'll crack up.

Why did the cookie lose the
spelling bee?
It crumbled under pressure.

What did the baker say to the bread?
Let's rise early.

What didn't the Teddy Bear have dessert?
Because he was stuffed!

Why was the fish afraid to write
the movie review?
It was on a scale of 1 to 10.

Why did the chicken smell?
Because it was fowl.

Why can you always trust a mouse?
Cause he ain't no rat!

How do elephants get ready
for a vacation?
They pack their trunk.

What do squirrels take so many risks?
They're used to going out on a limb.

Why did the bird get so mad
at the wind?
It really ruffled his feathers.

Why wouldn't the horse stop talking?
He was stalling.

What do oceans eat?
Sandwiches.

Why are eggs unreliable during
stressful situations?
They always crack under pressure.

How did the punch go over
at the party?
It was a hit!

What happened to the
World Sugar Association?
It eventually dissolved.

Why was everyone laughing at the egg?
Because he was yoking around.

Why did the recipe hurt?
It called for a pinch of salt.

What did the lid say when asked about
how it was handling the situation?
"Don't worry, I'm on top of it!"

Have you tried the new
jam-and-jelly buffet?
They have a lovely spread.

Why did the cat want everyone to
try her brownies?
Because she made them from scratch.

Why was the knife being so nice to
the toast?
To butter him up

What did the parmesan say to
the cheddar?
Good things come to those who grate

Why don't people like spicy peppers?
Because they get jalapeno business.

What is a can of soda's favorite
type of music?
Pop.

Why was the jar of jelly late to work?
There was a bit of a jam.

What did one nut say to the other when
they were playing tag?
"I'm gonna cashew!"

Was it hard for the baker to cut
through the dessert?
No, it was a piece of cake.

What's wrong with the jokes
cheddar makes?
They're too cheesy.

How does a train eat its food?
It chew-chews.

Where does winter go for summer vacation?
Iceland.

What should you drink if you're coming down with a cold?
Cough-ee

What do bakers plant in their gardens?
Flour

Why'd the sheep get put into time out?
He was being BAADDDD

How did the paper always get in front of the line?
He paper cut.

Why did the bucket go to the doctor?
He was a little pail

When's the best time to go to the
Renaissance fair?
Knight-time

What do you call a smart piece
of bread?
An honor roll

What did the cat say when his tail
got stepped on?
Me-OW!

What's a cactus' favorite thing to eat?
Desert

Why was the firework factory owner
so happy?
Business was booming!

How come the old dog was depressed?
He'd had a ruff life.

What was the problem at the animal's
elementary school?
No one wanted to sit next to
the cheetah (cheater)

What does Superman use to clean up
after his dog, Krypto?
A super duper pooper scooper

What did the moon say when it was
breaking up with the earth?
I'm over you!

What happens to an orange if it gets a sunburn?

It starts to peel.

Why don't eggs go to the tanning salon?

They don't want to get fried.

Kid #1: Tell me your favorite vegetable.
Kid #2: Peas.
Kid #1: Sorry. Tell me your favorite vegetable, PLEASE.

Why was the peanut butter sandwich late to work?

It got stuck in a traffic jam.

How did the pirate do in school?
Not well.. he was a sea student

What's a chip's favorite type of dance?
The salsa

What does an elephant wear
to the beach?
Swim trunks

What does baby bubble call
daddy bubble?
Pop.

Did you hear about the guy stealing
people's coffee cups?
They arrested him and took his MUG shot!

Why was the tennis supply factory so noisy?
Because they were always making a racket.

Why did the man have music coming from his shoe?
He had a club foot.

Why did the bathtub need to take a nap?
Because he was drained.

Why did the cowboy get a wiener dog?
Someone told him to "get a long little doggie."

Why was the car so embarrassed?
It was filled up with gas.

What goes "clomp, clomp, clomp, clomp, clomp, clomp, clomp, pff"?

A spider with a shoe missing.

Why are doughnuts so good at golf?

Because they always have a hole in one.

How did the ray-gun tell the spaceman he was stinky?

Pew! Pew! Pew! Pee-yu!

How many cavemen does it take to screw in a lightbulb?

None, silly, cavemen don't have electricity!

CPSIA information can be obtained
at www.ICGtesting.com
Printed in the USA
LVHW100947291121
704728LV00016B/821

9 781942 915331